ALGERIA

...in Pictures

Photo by Bernice K. Condit

Visual Geography Series®

ALGERIA

...in Pictures

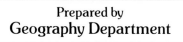

Prepared by
Geography Department

Lerner Publications Company
Minneapolis

Photo by Bernice K. Condit

Boys gather for a game of football (soccer) in the northern Algerian town of Bordj Bou Arreridj.

This book is a newly commissioned title in the Visual Geography Series. The text is set in 10/12 Century Textbook.

LIBRARY OF CONGRESS CATALOGING-IN-PUBLICATION DATA

Algeria in pictures / prepared by Geography Department, Lerner Publications Company, Minneapolis.
   p. cm. — (Visual geography series)
   Includes index.
   Summary: Describes the topography, history, society, economy, and governmental structure of Algeria.
   ISBN 0-8225-1901-1 (lib. bdg.)
   1. Algeria. [1. Algeria.]   I. Lerner Publications Company. Geography Dept. II. Series: Visual geography series (Minneapolis, Minn.).
   DT275.A57724 1992
   965—dc20   91–30722
                                                         CIP
                                                          AC

International Standard Book Number: 0-8225-1901-1
Library of Congress Card Catalog Number: 91-30722

VISUAL GEOGRAPHY SERIES®

Publisher
Harry Jonas Lerner
Senior Editor
Mary M. Rodgers
Editors
Gretchen Bratvold
Tom Streissguth
Photo Researcher
Bill Kauffmann
Editorial/Photo Assistants
Marybeth Campbell
Colleen Sexton
Consultants/Contributors
James P. Johnson
Sandra K. Davis
Designer
Jim Simondet
Cartographer
Carol F. Barrett
Indexers
Kristine S. Schubert
Sylvia Timian
Production Manager
Gary J. Hansen

Photo by Daniel H. Condit

High stone walls once protected the northwestern Algerian city of Tlemcen.

Acknowledgments

Title page photo © Jane Thomas/Visuals Unlimited.

Elevation contours adapted from *The Times Atlas of the World,* seventh comprehensive edition (New York: Times Books, 1985).

1 2 3 4 5 6 7 8 9 10 01 00 99 98 97 96 95 94 93 92

Photo by Daniel H. Condit

At this shop in Algiers, the capital of Algeria, merchants offer a variety of household goods to passing shoppers. The city has been an important North African trading center since the sixteenth century.

Contents

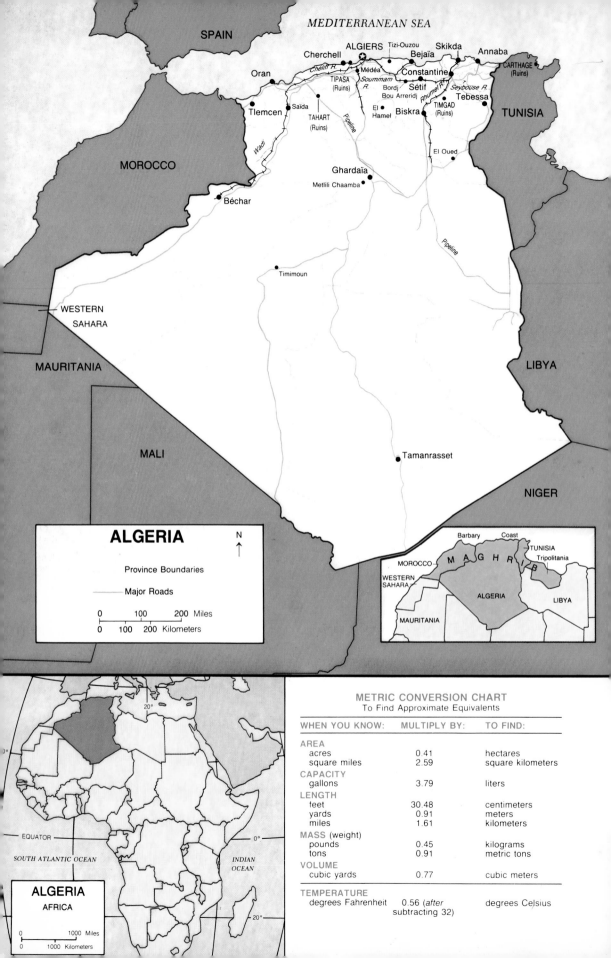

MEDITERRANEAN SEA

SPAIN

ALGIERS
Cherchell   Tizi-Ouzou   Skikda
Bejaïa   Annaba
Médéa   Constantine   CARTHAGE
Oran   TIPASA   Soummam   Sétif   (Ruins)
(Ruins)   R.   Bordj   Rhumel R.   Seybouse R.
Chélili R.   Bou Arreridj   TIMGAD   Tebessa
Tlemcen   Saïda   (Ruins)   TUNISIA
El   Biskra
TAHART   Hamel
(Ruins)

MOROCCO   El Oued

Ghardaïa
Metlili Chaamba
Béchar

Pipeline

Timimoun

WESTERN
SAHARA

MAURITANIA   LIBYA

MALI

Tamanrasset

NIGER

ALGERIA

N
↑

Province Boundaries

——— Major Roads

0   100   200 Miles
0   100   200 Kilometers

MAGHRIB

Barbary   Coast
TUNISIA
MOROCCO   Tripolitania
WESTERN
SAHARA   ALGERIA   LIBYA

MAURITANIA

20°

EQUATOR   0°

SOUTH ATLANTIC OCEAN   INDIAN
OCEAN
20°

ALGERIA
AFRICA

0   1000 Miles
0   1000 Kilometers

METRIC CONVERSION CHART
To Find Approximate Equivalents

WHEN YOU KNOW:	MULTIPLY BY:	TO FIND:
AREA		
acres	0.41	hectares
square miles	2.59	square kilometers
CAPACITY		
gallons	3.79	liters
LENGTH		
feet	30.48	centimeters
yards	0.91	meters
miles	1.61	kilometers
MASS (weight)		
pounds	0.45	kilograms
tons	0.91	metric tons
VOLUME		
cubic yards	0.77	cubic meters
TEMPERATURE		
degrees Fahrenheit	0.56 (after subtracting 32)	degrees Celsius

Ghardaïa is the principal city of the Mzab region in the northern Sahara Desert. The Mzab is famous for the unique architectural style of its public buildings and private homes.

Introduction

Algeria, a large North African nation of 26 million people, stretches from the vast Sahara Desert to the Mediterranean Sea. The country benefits from productive farmland as well as extensive natural resources. Algeria has also become a political leader in Africa and among the world's developing nations. Yet, since gaining independence from French rule in 1962, Algeria has struggled to provide economic progress for its people.

Algeria's earliest inhabitants were wandering herders and hunters who did not build permanent settlements. The first large towns in the region were trading posts set up along the Mediterranean coast

7

by European and Middle Eastern peoples. Eventually, these settlers developed larger cities and farming estates in the fertile plains and mountain valleys of northern Algeria.

During most of its history, Algeria has not been culturally or politically unified. An invasion by Middle Eastern Arabs in the seventh century A.D. brought a new religion—Islam—whose followers are called Muslims. Although Islam spread rapidly among the inhabitants of both coastal and desert areas, new sects of the religion competed fiercely for land and trade. For centuries after the Arab conquest, rival Islamic dynasties, from the Middle East, from Spain, and from other areas of North Africa, controlled various cities and regions of Algeria.

In the sixteenth century, the coast of Algeria was conquered by the Ottoman Turks, whose realm lay in what is now Turkey. While under Ottoman control, Algeria's coastal cities became safe harbors for pirates who attacked and plundered ships on the high seas. By the early nineteenth century, piracy had brought several European nations into conflict with the country's rulers. In 1830 French forces invaded Algiers, now the capital of Algeria. Eventually most of northern Algeria became part of France.

The French built new industries and an extensive road system in Algeria. But *colons*—settlers who arrived from France, Italy, and Spain—denied most Muslims any role in Algeria's government. In addition, the colons allowed few Muslims to

These young men are selling fresh vegetables in a *suq* (public market) in the city of Oran. Other suq vendors may offer food, crafts, jewelry, or live animals for sale.

Workers measure cedar trunks that will be cut into lumber at a busy sawmill. Timber cutting has depleted many of Algeria's forested areas, but the Algerian government has developed an extensive reforestation program.

own land or to run businesses. This situation led to a bloody civil war that ended in 1962 when Muslim Algerians formed an independent republic.

Algeria spent many years recovering from the war and from the departure of skilled teachers, engineers, and technicians after the war. In the 1960s, the National Liberation Front (FLN), the leading Muslim faction in the civil war, took over the Algerian government and made all opposing political parties illegal. FLN leaders also put into place a tightly controlled economy.

Support for the FLN began to decline in the 1980s, after many years of high unemployment and economic weakness. Under pressure from opposition parties, the FLN allowed non-FLN politicians to run for office in the early 1990s. In January 1992, an election victory by FLN opponents prompted the military to oust Algeria's president and replace him with a five-member High State Council. The government's instability underlines the difficulties Algerians face in developing both democracy and a more successful economy.

This mosque (Islamic house of prayer) in downtown Algiers was once a Roman Catholic cathedral. The architects who converted the cathedral added pointed arches and minarets (towers) to the front of the structure.

The highlands of the Great Kabylia Mountains near the city of Constantine afford spectacular views over the surrounding countryside.

1) The Land

Algeria lies in the Maghrib region of northwestern Africa. Other countries in the Maghrib include Morocco, which is west of Algeria, and Tunisia and Libya, which are situated to the east. The Mediterranean Sea forms Algeria's northern coast. Mauritania and Mali border Algeria to the southwest, and Niger lies to the southeast. The second largest African country, Algeria has a land area of 919,595 square miles, making it more than three times the size of Texas.

Small, rocky islands off its northern shores inspired Algeria's name—*al-Jazair,* meaning "the islands" in Arabic, the language of modern Algerians. The 750-mile Mediterranean coastline was the site of the region's first ports and trading settlements. Under French rule, European designers planned new neighborhoods and industries in the northern cities. Most population centers, farms, and factories still lie on or near the coast.

The Algerian interior consists of mountains, basins (low, flat regions), high plateaus, and part of the dry and hot Sahara Desert. Soil erosion and drought have allowed the Sahara to advance gradually northward, and the desert now covers more than 80 percent of Algeria's land.

Topography

The Tell, Algeria's northernmost region, stretches in a band 80 to 200 miles wide along the Mediterranean coast. In the Tell, narrow plains lie between the sea and a series of mountain ranges. Short river valleys in these highlands provide fertile soil for vineyards, olive groves, and wheat fields.

An extension of the Atlas Mountains of Morocco, the Tell Atlas consists of a series of ranges spanning northern Algeria as far east as Tunisia. Between the ranges are dry basins, fertile valleys, and plains. The Great Kabylia Mountains rise south and east of Algiers. The Little Kabylia Mountains lie between the Soummam River, east of Algiers, and the port of Skikda. The Medjerda range, east of the city of Constantine, runs northeastward across the Tunisian border.

Photo by Jaap Verschoor, Haarlem, the Netherlands

Although an extremely hot and dry environment, the Sahara Desert supports scrub vegetation and hardy date palms.

Photo by Daniel H. Condit

The Djurdjura Mountains tower above a fertile plain in northeastern Algeria. This range is an extension of the Atlas Mountains, which stretch across Algeria and Morocco.

11

The Ahaggar Mountains are rugged and barren highlands near Algeria's border with Libya. Travel through the area is difficult, because few roads are paved and little water or shelter is available.

South of the Tell, the dry, rolling plains of the High Plateau vary from 1,300 to 4,300 feet in elevation. To the south and west, these plains rise gradually to the Saharan Atlas range. Higher than the Tell Atlas, the Saharan Atlas Mountains run from the Moroccan frontier to the desert town of Biskra.

Flat salt basins called *chotts* are an important feature of the High Plateau. The chotts become shallow lakes during the rare rains in the region. Chott Melrhir, near the Tunisian border, reaches Algeria's lowest elevation—102 feet below sea level. Just north of Chott Melrhir are the Aurès Mountains, which are high enough to receive occasional snowfalls during Algeria's short winter season.

The Algerian Sahara begins south of the Saharan Atlas and extends southward as far as the country's borders with Mali and Niger. Lying in the northern Sahara are the Great Western and Great Eastern ergs —vast, barren regions of sand and gravel. Between the ergs rises the Mzab, a rocky limestone plateau. Desert oases—small fertile areas that draw their water from underground reservoirs—are scattered throughout the Sahara.

With limited water sources and little fertile soil, the southern Sahara supports only a few small towns and a declining population of nomadic peoples. Most roads in the region are bumpy tracks that are frequently buried under the desert's shifting sands. Iguidi Erg and Chech Erg straddle the Mauritanian and Malian borders, respectively. The Tassili N'Ajjer Mountains, a remote range in the southeastern Sahara, rises near Libya. The Ahaggar Mountains farther south include Mount Tahat (9,852 feet), the highest point in Algeria.

Rivers

Algeria has limited water resources and no navigable rivers. Most streams in the Tell region run northward to the coast of the Mediterranean Sea through narrow mountain passes. Dams built on some of these waterways provide irrigation for farms in the region.

The 450-mile Chéliff River is the country's longest waterway. Rising in the Tell Atlas south of Algiers, the Chéliff turns sharply westward before emptying into the Mediterranean east of the port of Oran. Separating the Great Kabylia and Little Kabylia ranges, the Soummam River reaches the Mediterranean near the harbor town of Bejaïa. The Seybouse River, 145 miles in length, originates in the Medjer-da range and waters a level plain south of Annaba, Algeria's busiest port.

No permanent rivers exist south of the Tell Atlas. During the rainy season in the High Plateau, temporary streams run through *wadis* (natural riverbeds). Most of these streams empty into the low-lying, salty chotts. A few small rivers also flow during the rainy season in the higher elevations of the Saharan Atlas. To the south, underground sources provide much-needed drinking water and irrigation in the oases of the Sahara Desert.

Climate

During most of the year, Algeria has a hot and dry climate. Northern winds that blow

A bridge crosses the deep Rhumel Gorge near Constantine. Located in the Tell Atlas Mountains, Constantine sits on top of a steep chalk cliff that overlooks the Rhumel, a small and swift watercourse.

Photo by Bernice K. Condit

in winter and spring bring occasional rainfall, much of which falls in the country's higher elevations. The basins and valleys near Algeria's Mediterranean coast have warm, dry summers and mild winters.

Annual rainfall in the Tell varies from 16 to 39 inches, depending on elevation. Temperatures in the region average 78° F during the summer, and 50° F during the winter. Hot, dusty summer winds called siroccos sweep northward from the Sahara across the Tell. These winds can create sandstorms that travel across the Mediterranean and as far as southern Europe.

The High Plateau receives most of its annual rainfall—which averages 8 to 16 inches—from September through December. In these months, winds shift from the east and northeast to the west and north. During the rest of the year, drought conditions prevail on the High Plateau. Temperatures in the region average 81° F in the summer months and 40° F during the winter.

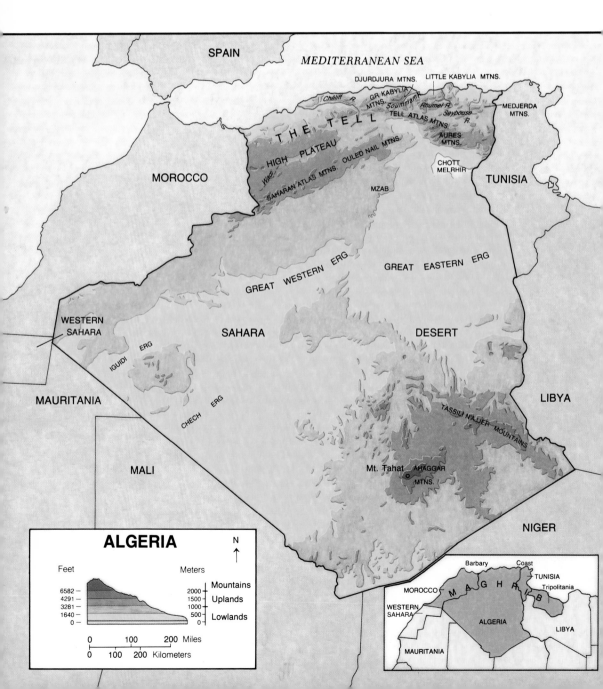

Farther south, the Sahara Desert experiences extremes in temperature and very low humidity. Nights in the desert can be near freezing, while midday temperatures often reach 120° F. Average annual rainfall in the Sahara is less than five inches, and some areas receive no rain for years.

Flora and Fauna

Overgrazing, extensive tree cutting, and uncontrolled forest fires have drastically reduced Algeria's forested areas, which now cover about 1 percent of the country's land. Most coastal plains and valleys support only sparse natural vegetation. In mountainous and well-watered regions of the Tell, deciduous (leaf-shedding) trees such as oak survive. Atlas cedar and Aleppo pine, which can thrive in dry climates, are also common.

Esparto grass and brushwood flourish in the flat basins of the High Plateau. Acacia trees, jujube trees, and scrub vegetation grow on the northern plains of the Sahara. South of the Saharan Atlas, vegetation adapted to arid conditions survives near dry riverbeds. Date palms draw water from underground sources in the oases.

In the 1970s, the Algerian government began a program of reforestation to slow the northward spread of the Sahara. Workers planted millions of pine and cypress trees to prevent erosion and to serve as a barrier against the spreading sand dunes. Continued drought and overgrazing, however, have hampered the success of this program.

Centuries of unrestricted hunting has eliminated most Algerian wildlife. A small number of antelope still live in remote mountainous regions. Hares and gazelles also survive in the Tell. Snakes, lizards, hyenas, jackals, and vultures inhabit the Sahara. Many people living in the desert use camels—which can survive for long periods on little water—as a means of transportation.

Photo by Jak Kilby

In the arid desert, vegetation is thickest in the seasonal watercourses known as *wadis.* This wadi in southern Algeria supports mimosa trees, cacti, low shrubs, and broad-leafed plants.

Photo © Irma Turtle

The Tuareg—a seminomadic desert people of southern Algeria—travel the long distances of the Sahara by camel.

Natural Resources

Despite its rugged and largely barren terrain, Algeria is rich in minerals and energy resources. The discovery of large oil deposits in the eastern Sahara in the 1950s created a vital source of export earnings. Extensive natural gas fields also exist in the northwestern Sahara. Pipelines that transport natural gas and oil run northward from these fields to ports on the Mediterranean coast.

Large reserves of phosphate, an important ingredient of agricultural fertilizer, have been found near the Tunisian border. Nearby deposits of iron ore and coal supply Algeria's steel industry. Other Algerian minerals include lead, zinc, and mercury.

These materials are valuable in manufacturing and as exports.

Deposits of uranium, which is used in generating nuclear energy, lie near Tamanrasset in the southern Sahara. The country's limited forests, half of which are owned by the Algerian government, provide hardwood, cork, and cordage (material used to make rope).

Cities

Algeria's largest cities have grown along or near the country's Mediterranean coastline. Trade and industry thrive near the ports, from which companies export raw materials, crude and refined oil, natural

At a large nursery near Constantine, workers prepare pine, eucalyptus, acacia, and cedar saplings (young trees) for replanting in the northern Sahara Desert. Through its reforestation efforts, the Algerian government is attempting to stop soil erosion and the steady advance of the desert toward fertile areas in northern Algeria.

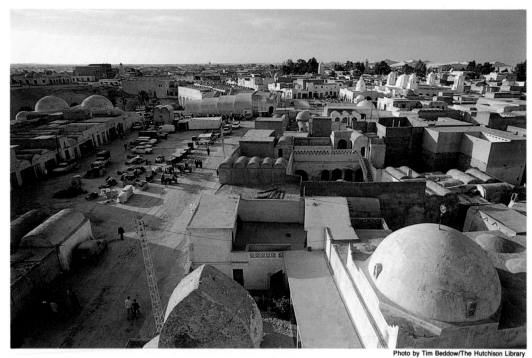

The town of El Oued lies north of the Great Eastern Erg, a barren plain of sand and rock near Algeria's border with Tunisia. The town's residents designed many buildings with domes and barrel-shaped roofs to lessen the desert's intense heat.

gas, and finished goods. Smaller cities of the interior developed near water sources and along ancient trade routes. Since the country's independence in 1962, many people from poorer rural areas have moved to the northern cities in search of jobs and housing. The result has been growing unemployment and urban overcrowding.

ALGIERS

Algeria's capital and largest city, Algiers (population 1.5 million) is also an important Mediterranean seaport. The city's oldest sections rise on a steep hill to the west of a spacious harbor. First settled by Phoenician traders in the twelfth century B.C., Algiers later was home to Romans

Many large apartment buildings in Algiers date to the nineteenth and early twentieth centuries, when the northern part of the country was under French control.

Photo by Bernice K. Condit

Like many cities in North Africa, Constantine has an old central neighborhood—known as a *medina*—and a large surrounding area *(above)* with wide roads, heavy motor traffic, and newer buildings.

from the Italian Peninsula and Berbers from the Sahara. From the fifteenth until the eighteenth centuries A.D., pirates sailed from Algiers to raid commercial shipping. In the 1830s, the city came under French control, which ended in 1962.

The presidential palace, government offices, court buildings, and several national museums line the wide boulevards near the harbor of Algiers. The city streets become narrow, winding alleys in the Casba, an old quarter built on the ruins of a sixteenth-century fortress. The rapid population growth in Algiers after World War II (1939–1945) led to the establishment of many new suburbs on the hills that lie west of the city.

Companies based in Algiers export a wide variety of agricultural and industrial goods. Important industries in the city include cement factories, chemical plants, and paper mills. Algiers has also benefited from the development of crude oil and natural gas deposits in the Sahara.

Businesses that own pipelines, oil tankers, and refineries in the port employ many local workers. The city has become the hub of Algeria's railroad and highway networks and is also the site of the country's busiest international airport.

SECONDARY CITIES

Oran (population 629,000), Algeria's second largest city, lies on a wide harbor 225 miles southwest of Algiers. First settled in the tenth century, Oran came under direct Spanish rule in the sixteenth century. The port and the city were rebuilt after a devastating earthquake in 1790. Under French occupation, which began in 1831, European architects and engineers designed large houses and tree-lined boulevards in the city's center.

Oran exports produce—including wine, cereals, fruit, and vegetables—from the farms of western Algeria. Many nations in western Africa trade with Oran and ship their goods through this port. Factories in

Photo by Bernice K. Condit

Apartment houses cling to a steep cliff in Constantine. Known as Cirta to the ancient Berbers who inhabited the site, Constantine had imposing defenses that made it an important stronghold in northeastern Algeria.

Photo by Daniel H. Condit

Residents walk a busy side street in downtown Algiers. The country's capital is also an important commercial center and the busiest port in the Maghrib region, which includes Morocco, Algeria, and Tunisia.

and near Oran make carpets, textiles, beverages, and machinery. The city's harbor also contains extensive facilities for ship-building and ship repair.

Built on a rocky hilltop, Constantine (population 441,000) was once the city of Cirta, the capital of an ancient Berber kingdom. The settlement was later renamed for a Roman emperor who reigned during the third and fourth centuries A.D. Constantine came under French control in 1837. Like many urban centers in North Africa, Constantine has a small, older neighborhood surrounded by a modern section of wide streets and nineteenth-

century buildings. Constantine's major industries manufacture leather items and cloth goods.

Annaba (population 306,000) is a busy port located 70 miles northeast of Constantine. The city began as Hippo Regius, a Roman settlement that flourished until the fourth century A.D. During its history, Annaba has also been under Berber, Arab, Italian, Spanish, and French rule. The elaborate ruins of the old Roman city still attract tourists to Annaba. Minerals and agricultural goods are exported from the port, which also has a naval base, a large steelworks, and a chemical plant.

Photo by Daniel H. Condit

Modern buildings rise in the port of Oran, which lies on Algeria's Mediterranean seacoast. Once controlled by the Spanish, Oran was the capital of a French *departement* (province) before Algeria's independence in 1962.

Photo by Science VU/Visuals Unlimited

These vivid cave paintings in southern Algeria show ancient inhabitants of the region with a herd of cattle. Although now hot, dry, and largely barren, the Sahara once had enough rainfall and vegetation to support crops and cattle.

2) History and Government

Thousands of years ago, the vast Sahara Desert was a savanna—or grassland—with plentiful wildlife and a mild climate. In the Tassili N'Ajjer Mountains in southeastern Algeria, thousands of ancient rock paintings depict humans hunting antelope and elephants in the nearby savanna. Some of these paintings date as far back as 8000 B.C. Later paintings show that inhabitants of the region also raised cattle and crops.

By 4000 B.C., however, a drastic climatic change was taking place throughout northern Africa. Rainfall in the Sahara lessened, causing streams and lakes to dry up and

topsoil to erode. The inhabitants of the region began moving to more fertile areas to the north and east. In northern Algeria, the migrating hunters and farmers met a nomadic desert people whom Europeans later called Berbers.

The Berbers, whose origins are unknown, shared a common language. Their society was divided into many independent clans made up of several Berber families, who moved from place to place in search of pasture and game. The clans often combined into larger groups for mutual defense. Some Berber groups remained united long enough to establish control over large

21

Stone masons carved this image of a Phoenician ship into an ancient slab. Accomplished sailors and merchants, the Phoenicians established trading ports in Algeria and Tunisia before 1000 B.C.

areas of North Africa. Few ancient Berber leaders, however, established lasting states or boundaries in Algeria.

In the twelfth century B.C., seagoing Phoenician traders from the Middle East built outposts along Africa's Mediterranean coast. These merchants soon made contact with the Berbers and began trading with nomads who roamed the region south of the Tell. The largest Phoenician outpost, Carthage (in what is now Tunisia), eventually became North Africa's wealthiest ancient city. With a large merchant navy, Carthage eventually extended its control over much of North Africa.

Carthaginians and Berbers cooperated to protect their valuable trade. The Carthaginians paid Berber soldiers to defend Carthaginian cities against raids by nomadic peoples from the interior. By the third century B.C., Carthage was coming under attack by the armies of Rome, a

Carthage, the largest Phoenician port in the Mediterranean, grew into a wealthy and powerful North African empire. The Carthaginian commander Hannibal marched through Spain, southern France, and Italy to confront Roman forces during the Punic Wars. Hannibal used elephants—seen here rafting across France's Rhone River—to break through enemy lines. Despite his tactics, Hannibal suffered defeat in Italy, and the Romans later destroyed Carthage.

Photo by Daniel H. Condit

The Roman emperor Caracalla raised this triumphal arch in the ancient city of Tebessa in A.D. 214. In the sixth century, when forces of the Byzantine Empire were conquering cities and ports in North Africa, a Byzantine general incorporated the arch into a protective wall that encircled the city.

republic of southern Italy that was rapidly conquering territory in the Mediterranean region.

Roman Rule

The conflict between Rome and Carthage later erupted into a series of wars. After fighting battles in both Europe and Africa, Rome's stronger armies defeated the Carthaginians. In the second century B.C., the Romans destroyed the city of Carthage. The Romans built new cities at Timgad, in the Aurès Mountains, and at Tebessa, southeast of Constantine.

A Berber leader, Masinissa, had formed an alliance with Carthage but later switched his loyalty to Rome. After the defeat of the Carthaginians, Masinissa established his capital at Cirta (modern Constantine) and extended his rule over much of North Africa. After Masinissa's death, his heirs continued to rule this realm, which the Romans called Numidia.

Masinissa's grandson Jugurtha carried out a long campaign against Roman armies but was defeated in 106 B.C. The Romans later made Numidia a colony, dividing the territory into provinces that were administered by military governors.

After the defeat of Jugurtha, Roman settlers built towns and large farming estates in the region. The inhabitants of these Numidian cities spoke Latin—Rome's language—and were subject to Roman laws. A network of aqueducts (structures used to transport water) and roads helped the colony's trade and agriculture to flourish. Berber farmers rented land from the Romans, making their rental payments in grain. To ease the shipment of the region's large crop harvests to Italy, the Romans rebuilt the port of Carthage. Eventually Numidia was supplying much of Rome's grain.

For several centuries, Numidia remained a secure and prosperous Roman province. Yet events in other parts of the Roman

23

The ruins of a Roman house at Tipasa lie near the Mediterranean seacoast west of Algiers. Tipasa was a prosperous port under Roman rule and later became an important center of the Christian faith.

Empire affected the region. Conflict with peoples living near the Roman frontiers was weakening the empire's defenses. In addition, Christianity—a religion that began in the Roman province of Palestine (modern Israel)—was gaining followers in Numidian cities and among the nomadic Berbers. Many of the new Christians in North Africa joined a growing movement for independence from Rome.

Vandal Invasions

Although the emperor Constantine made Christianity Rome's official religion, the independence movement against Roman rule in Numidia remained strong. The Berbers who adopted Christianity formed new religious groups, such as the Donatists, to resist control of their church by Roman clergy.

Augustine, the Christian bishop of Hippo Regius (the modern city of Annaba), preached against Donatism. In his writings, Augustine also warned that Rome's African colonies were vulnerable to attack. Just after Augustine's death in A.D. 429, Hippo Regius and much of Numidia were overrun by the Vandals, a northern European people who had invaded North Africa from Spain.

After making Carthage their capital, the Vandals took over trade with Europe and with African peoples living to the south. Vandal leaders still allowed Roman officials to administer Numidia, but Roman military power was declining, and much of the region fell into disorder.

The nomadic peoples who roamed the dry plains south of the Tell set up new trade routes across the Sahara. Traveling in groups called caravans, the nomads controlled the valuable trade in gold and other goods across the desert. These peoples formed new alliances among themselves to maintain their independence.

The Vandals held the coast of North Africa until the early sixth century, when Byzantine forces from eastern Europe arrived. A wealthy and militarily strong state, the Byzantine Empire sought control of North African ports. But Byzantine authority in Algeria lasted only until the mid-seventh century, when Arabs from the Middle East invaded North Africa.

The Arab Conquest

The Arabs brought Islam, a new religion, to Algeria. The followers of Islam—called Muslims—believed in the word of God, as revealed to the Arab prophet Muhammad. Muslims considered Islamic law the source of religious and civil authority.

In the century following Muhammad's death in 632, the Muslim Arabs conquered most of North Africa. Although many inhabitants of Algeria resisted the Arab invasions, others accepted the new rulers and converted to Islam. In certain regions, such as in the Kabylia and Aurès mountains, Berber clans remained independent.

In the eighth century, North Africa —including much of present-day Morocco,

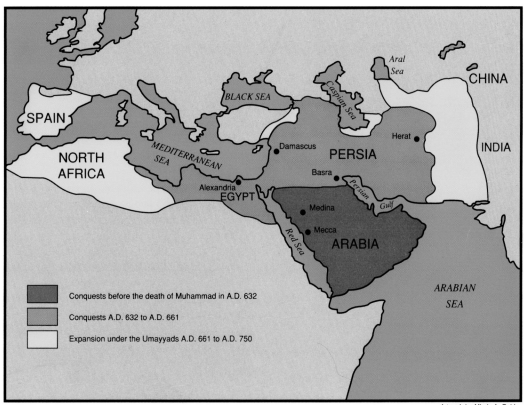

Artwork by Mindy A. Rabin

After the death in A.D. 632 of Muhammad, the founder of the Islamic religion, Arab armies swept through the Middle East and North Africa. The Arabs had conquered much of northern Algeria by the late seventh century. Although many people in the Maghrib resisted these invasions, Arabs settled along the Mediterranean coast and eventually converted many of Algeria's Berbers to Islam.

Libya, Tunisia, and Algeria—came under the control of the Abbasid dynasty (family of rulers) of Baghdad (in modern Iraq). These Arabs, who had also conquered much of Spain, knew the entire western portion of their domain as the Maghrib, meaning "the west" in the Arabic language.

Abbasid control of the Algerian seacoast provided security for the region's port towns, which still traded actively with the Middle East and with Europe. Arabic-speaking merchants on the coast formed partnerships with the Berbers of the interior. In addition, religious instruction was carried out in classical Arabic, the language of the Koran, or Islamic holy book. This contact gradually spread the Arabic language to Berbers living in towns along the seacoast and in the larger cities of the interior.

BERBER DYNASTIES

Not all Berber clans accepted Arab rule or the traditional form of Islam. In 739 a Berber revolt in neighboring Morocco spread to Algeria. Several Berber kingdoms that had established new Islamic sects rose to oppose Abbasid rule. The Rustimid dynasty at Tahart, about 100 miles southeast of Oran, became one of the most powerful of these Berber realms. The city of Tahart, which controlled many important caravan routes, soon was flourishing from trade in gold and grain. By the late eighth century, the Abbasids no longer ruled the Algerian Berbers.

In the late 800s, Berbers from the Kabylia region led a successful crusade against the Abbasid rulers in Tunisia. These Berbers later installed a new Arab dynasty known as the Fatimids. The Fatimids then turned westward, conquering Tahart and driving the followers of the Rustimid dynasty southward beyond the Tell Atlas Mountains.

Rebellion broke out among the Berbers in the late tenth century, after the Fatimids had moved their capital east to Cairo in Egypt. As Fatimid control weakened, the Berber clans switched their loyalties from the Arabs to local Berber chieftains. For two centuries, Algeria remained a chaotic region without central authority.

THE BEDOUIN AND ARAB BROTHERHOODS

In the eleventh century, the Fatimids attempted to reestablish control over Algeria by inviting Arab nomads—known as Bedouin—to migrate from the Middle East to North Africa. The Bedouin devastated cities and farms, forcing many Ber-

Courtesy of Cultural and Tourism Office of the Turkish Embassy

Illustrators used elaborate Arabic script on this page of the Koran, the Islamic holy book. Arabic became the most important tongue in North Africa through its use by scholars, merchants, administrators, and Islamic clergy.

This nobleman was a member of the Hafsid dynasty, a family of rulers from Tunisia. The Hafsids, who took control of much of eastern Algeria in the early 1200s, were among the first North African dynasties to establish diplomatic relations with European states.

bers from their lands. Eventually, however, the Bedouin peoples settled in northern Algeria, intermarrying with the Berbers and further spreading the Arabic language through the region.

About the same time as the Bedouin migrations, new Islamic groups were gaining followers among the Berbers. These groups rallied around Islamic holy men, established semimilitary orders, and demanded a strict observance of Islamic law. One such group, the Almoravids, originated in the southwestern Sahara. The Almoravids swept northward and by the late eleventh century had brought many Algerian cities under their control.

Another group of Islamic reformers known as the Almohads, who lived in the rugged Atlas Mountains of Morocco, opposed the Almoravids. By the mid-twelfth century, the Almohads had replaced the Almoravids as rulers of a Berber state that covered the Maghrib. The Almohad center at Tlemcen in northwestern Algeria grew wealthy by controlling the trade that passed through Algeria's ports. But Almohad authority in eastern Algeria gradually weakened, and by the 1200s this region was governed by the Hafsids, a powerful dynasty based in Tunisia.

In 1269 a new ruling group, the Zayanids, captured Tlemcen from the Almohads. Under the Zayanids, the city became one of northern Africa's richest urban centers. Tlemcen benefited from control of caravan routes in the Sahara and sea trade with southern Europe. Other Algerian cities and ports prospered during the Zayanid period. But Berber groups in the interior, many of them led by religious opponents of the Zayanids, retained their independence.

Suleyman I *(center left),* the sultan (ruler) of the Ottoman Empire, receives the pirate leader Khayr al-Din *(center right).* After Khayr al-Din captured Algiers in the 1500s and placed it under the sultan's control, Suleyman rewarded him with the title of *beylerby,* or governor, of the port. Algiers remained an important Ottoman possession until the 1800s.

Courtesy of Cultural and Tourism Office of the Turkish Embassy

Ottomans and Pirates

Raids by Europeans on the Mediterranean coast of the Maghrib had been common while the various Berber dynasties rose and fell from power in the region. In addition, North Africa became an important source of gold for the European states. After forcing Muslim leaders from Spain in 1492, Spanish Christians attacked and conquered several outposts along the African coast. The Spanish also captured an island fortress in the protected harbor of Algiers. As Muslims lost control of Spain to Christian rulers, refugees began to arrive in Algerian ports to assist in trade and piracy.

Spanish authority in North Africa suffered a severe blow in 1510, when Algiers was seized by Aruj and Khayr al-Din, Muslim brothers from the Greek island of Lesbos. Together they began raiding the surrounding countryside and attacking European ships in the Mediterranean.

After the death of his brother in 1518, Khayr al-Din, also known as Barbarossa ("red beard" in Italian), became commander of Algiers. He placed the city under the control of the Ottoman Empire, a Muslim realm that covered Asia Minor (modern Turkey) and much of the Middle East. In return, the Turkish sultan (ruler) of the Ottoman Empire appointed Khayr al-Din his *beylerby,* or representative, in Algiers.

Khayr al-Din quickly conquered the central coast of Algeria and eventually subdued much of North Africa. He grew wealthy from piracy at sea, which became a common occupation for ambitious Europeans who had moved to Algeria's ports.

The pirates, also known as corsairs, robbed trading ships and took hostages from captured vessels. Some captives became the slaves of merchants and officials in Algiers. Others were held in Algerian prisons until the pirates received a ransom payment. The corsairs voyaged as far as the coast of Iceland in the North Atlantic Ocean in search of plunder and prisoners.

After the death of Khayr al-Din in 1546, the Ottoman Turks took direct control of his realm. Turkish troops known as Janissaries were sent to protect the cities and to police the interior. The *aga,* or leader of the Janissaries, became the head of government in northern Algeria. The pirates, who made up a wealthy and powerful professional class, formed a guild (alliance) to protect their interests.

The Growth of Algiers

By 1600 Algiers had become the capital of what Europeans called the Barbary Coast. The port city profited from slave-trading and from ransoms paid by Europeans for hostages. Valuable goods, such as leather and horses, were exported from Algiers by Europeans operating in the Mediterranean region.

The lack of a strong central administration, however, eventually began to weaken the Ottoman Empire's hold on Algeria. Competition between corsairs, traders, and Turkish military leaders caused instability in the region. Various Berber groups living south of the coast threw their support to competing factions, while maintaining their own independence. By the late seventeenth century, the corsairs were challenging the Turkish sultan for control of Algiers. In 1671 the pirates ousted the Ottoman representative and replaced him with a *dey,* a ruler who had to be elected by the pirate guild. The Janissaries remained a strong military force. But the sultan, who ruled the empire from the distant city of Istanbul (in modern Turkey), began to lose influence over Algerian affairs.

Although they were elected for life, many of the deys were assassinated, and few exercised control beyond Algiers and the nearby countryside. In 1689 the right to elect the dey passed to the officers of the Janissaries. Strong competition between the pirates and the Janissaries gradually diminished the deys' authority.

In the late 1700s, pirate raids and the continuing ransom demands from the Barbary Coast provoked European states and the newly independent United States to

Courtesy of Library of Congress

Pirate raids disrupted shipping in the Mediterranean and in the Atlantic Ocean while North Africa was under Ottoman rule. Algiers, which lay at the center of North Africa's Barbary Coast, sheltered many pirates and supported a thriving trade in captives and stolen goods. But Algiers and other Barbary Coast ports came under attack from European and U.S. ships attempting to stop piracy in the late 1700s and early 1800s.

take action. These nations signed military agreements to prevent further raiding by the Barbary pirates.

In 1815 a U.S. force entered the harbor of Algiers, threatening the city with bombardment. The dey immediately agreed to end piracy, to release all captives, and to pay for damaged and stolen property. After the dey broke these promises, British, U.S., and Dutch ships arrived in Algiers in 1816 to enforce the agreement.

French Occupation

At the same time, relations between Algiers and France were worsening over a disputed shipment of Algerian grain. France refused to pay for the shipment unless Barbary Coast piracy ceased. In addition, having suffered a series of defeats in Europe, the French government sought to stop unrest at home by gaining a decisive military victory abroad. The conflict turned into an armed confrontation in 1830, when the French government sent forces to occupy Algiers. Four years later, France annexed much of northern Algeria as a colony.

The French occupation of Algeria spread out from Algiers to other coastal cities. French colonists, who were known as *colons,* seized farms and productive lands in the Tell. The colons forced many Muslim inhabitants to move to villages and farms in the dry and less fertile regions to the south. The Foreign Legion—an elite French

Photo by Bettmann Archive

In response to a dispute with the governor of Algiers, the French invaded North Africa in 1830. Although violent revolts broke out during the next decade, the French eventually brought all of Algeria under their control.

corps of professional soldiers equipped for desert warfare—built forts in Algeria to support and defend the colonists.

In the late 1830s, a movement to resist the French occupation formed around Abdelkader, the son of a popular Muslim religious leader. Abdelkader established an opposition government at Tlemcen and gained the support of the Muslim population living south of the Tell. He soon claimed all Algerian territory not directly controlled by French forces.

At first Abdelkader was able to wage an effective guerrilla war by attacking Foreign Legion outposts and the estates of the colons. But the French forces counterattacked, destroying rebellious villages and towns. As a stream of French reinforcements began arriving from Europe, many of the Muslim guerrillas abandoned the fight. In 1844, after Abdelkader had taken refuge in Morocco, the French entered that country and defeated the Moroccan army. Although he surrendered in 1847 and later was forced into exile, Abdelkader became the first hero of the independence movement among Algeria's Muslims.

European Settlement

In 1848 the French government made northern Algeria a part of France. Three provinces were created in the region, with their capitals at Oran, Algiers, and Constantine. The colons, who became the administrators of the provinces, built new schools, businesses, banks, and industries. Much of Algeria outside the provinces remained under military control. Muslims still made up a majority of the nation's population. But they could only attain citizenship in the new French territories by renouncing Islamic law and accepting the Napoleonic Code, the legal system of France. Very few Algerian Muslims were willing to take this step.

The arrival of settlers from France, Italy, and Spain in the nineteenth century led to further occupation of Muslim lands.

Photo by Mansell Collection

Abdelkader led an uprising in the 1830s and 1840s against the French. Although his revolt failed and he eventually surrendered, Abdelkader became an inspiring figure among Algerians who later fought for independence from France.

Some Europeans took farming estates by force. Others bought land and then sold it to settlers for a profit. To increase their authority, the colons sought to put all Algerian cities and estates under an independent civil administration. To achieve this goal, the colons opposed control of the colony by either the French military or by French government officials.

Many French leaders fought the actions of the colons. The French government passed measures to achieve fair land distribution between Muslims and settlers. But conflict within Algeria continued. In 1871 Muslim Algerians revolted against the colon administration in the independent Kabylia region. After the rebellion was put down, the French annexed

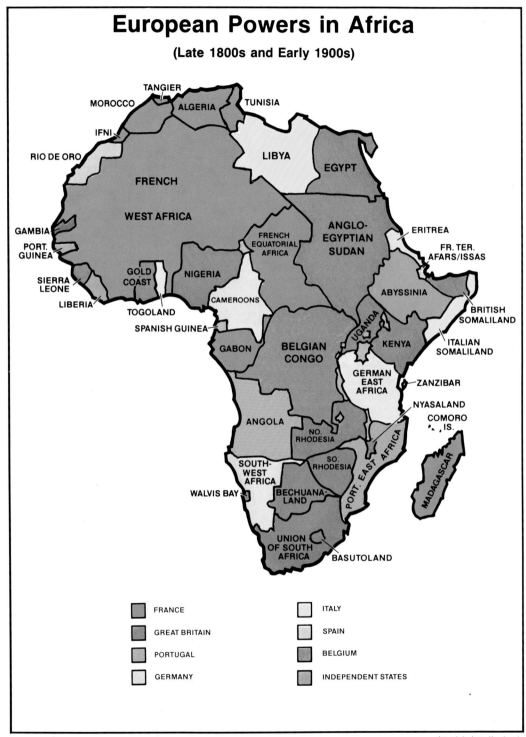

European Powers in Africa

(Late 1800s and Early 1900s)

TANGIER
MOROCCO
ALGERIA
TUNISIA
IFNI
RIO DE ORO
LIBYA
EGYPT
FRENCH
WEST AFRICA
FRENCH
EQUATORIAL
AFRICA
ANGLO-
EGYPTIAN
SUDAN
ERITREA
FR. TER.
AFARS/ISSAS
GAMBIA
PORT.
GUINEA
GOLD
COAST
NIGERIA
ABYSSINIA
SIERRA
LEONE
CAMEROONS
BRITISH
SOMALILAND
LIBERIA
TOGOLAND
UGANDA
KENYA
ITALIAN
SOMALILAND
SPANISH GUINEA
GABON
BELGIAN
CONGO
GERMAN
EAST
AFRICA
ZANZIBAR
NYASALAND
COMORO
IS.
ANGOLA
NO.
RHODESIA
SOUTH-
WEST
AFRICA
SO.
RHODESIA
PORT. EAST AFRICA
MADAGASCAR
WALVIS BAY
BECHUANA-
LAND
UNION
OF SOUTH
AFRICA
BASUTOLAND

FRANCE	ITALY
GREAT BRITAIN	SPAIN
PORTUGAL	BELGIUM
GERMANY	INDEPENDENT STATES

Artwork by Larry Kaushansky

By the late 1800s, European countries had divided the African continent into several areas of influence. **Northern Algeria included three provinces of France. The Sahara Desert region became part of French West Africa.** (Colonial map information taken from *The Anchor Atlas of World History*, 1978)

32

Muslim lands in the area and imposed strict laws on the inhabitants.

For the next few decades, Algeria experienced an uneasy peace between European colons and Algerian Muslims. These two groups were divided into separate societies, and little communication or intermarriage occurred between them. The leaders of the colons blocked any Muslim representation in the French parliament. Colon delegates also voted against any legislation that would ease Algeria's social and legal divisions.

The colons controlled Algeria's largest businesses and its foreign trade. A few Muslims who attended French universities returned to Algeria, forming a small professional class. By the early 1900s, however, the vast majority of Muslims still could not vote, could not move from their villages or towns, and could not take part in Algeria's government.

The Rise of Muslim Nationalism

In Europe at this time, conflict was brewing among several nations. France, Britain, and Russia had signed a treaty to oppose any aggression by Germany and its allies. World War I erupted when Germany invaded Belgium and France in the summer of 1914. France called upon Algeria and other French colonies to supply troops. More than 200,000 Algerian soldiers enlisted in the French army, eventually helping France and its allies to defeat Germany.

Algerians who returned home after the war ended in 1918 found a divided country in which Muslims still lacked both education and job opportunities. In their speeches and writings, Muslim religious leaders called for equality with Europeans in Algeria. Their demands for reform spurred a wave of nationalism among Muslim war veterans.

Photo by Bettmann Archive

Algeria's status as a part of France drew it into two world wars fought during the twentieth century. Many battles of World War I (1914–1918), which pitted France against Germany, were fought in northern France and Belgium. Here, members of the Algerian cavalry escort German prisoners to a base near the front lines.

In an attempt to shoot down German aircraft, gunners fire an artillery barrage skyward during a raid on Algiers in 1943. Some of the heaviest fighting of World War II occurred in North Africa, where German forces conquered several important Mediterranean ports.

During the 1920s, Algerian Muslims won some rights from the French government. More Muslims were allowed to become citizens, and Muslims joined advisory councils that operated in each Algerian province. The healthy economy of the 1920s improved living conditions for the colons and for some Muslims.

Yet the colons continued to resist reforms that would benefit Muslims. In response, Muslim leaders formed several groups that pressed for Algeria's complete independence from France. Abdelhamid Ben Badis began one such association in 1931. Another organization, headed by Ahmed Messali Hadj, was founded among North Africans who held jobs in France. After bringing his group to Algeria in 1937, Messali Hadj gained the support of Muslim workers and farmers.

The French government responded to the growing independence movement by proposing the Viollette Plan, which would extend citizenship to Muslim officials and professionals. Some Muslim leaders accepted the plan as a first step toward equality. Messali Hadj, who saw the plan as an attempt to divide Algerian Muslims, offered a plan of his own. It proposed voting rights for all Algerians and equality in wages, land distribution, and education. But colon representatives in the French parliament defeated all of these proposed reforms.

WORLD WAR II AND THE FLN

Another devastating world war broke out in Europe in the summer of 1939. Britain, France, and later the United States allied to oppose the Axis powers of Germany and Italy. France surrendered after a massive German invasion in the spring of 1940. A new French government that would cooperate with Germany was set up in the French town of Vichy. Algeria's administrators then came under the control of the Vichy government.

After France fell, Italy and Germany invaded North Africa. Tunisia, Libya, and a large part of Egypt came under the control of the Axis powers. To oppose this occupation, British, French, and U.S.

forces invaded Algeria in the fall of 1942, quickly defeating the country's pro-Vichy forces. Algeria became a base for Allied operations against Axis forces, which were driven from North Africa in 1943.

During the war, Messali Hadj and another prominent Muslim leader, Ferhat Abbas, demanded a new Algerian constitution and full legal equality for Muslims. The French government answered these demands by offering a new version of the Viollette Plan. But all negotiation stopped on May 8, 1945—the final day of World War II in Europe—when a victory celebration in Sétif, near Constantine, erupted into anti-European violence. More than 100 people were killed, touching off anti-Muslim riots throughout the country.

After the Sétif rioting, many Muslim leaders called for an armed revolt to establish an independent Muslim state in Algeria. Messali Hadj was arrested and deported to France, and other Muslim leaders went into exile. In Egypt the Algerian opposition leader Ahmed Ben Bella and several other Algerian exiles

formed a committee that later became the National Liberation Front (FLN).

After establishing a military branch, the FLN attacked French bases and communications centers in Algeria. The FLN also assassinated European and Muslim opponents of the independence movement. In response, armed colons attacked Muslim villages, destroying property and killing many of the inhabitants.

The War for Independence

To counter the violence, the French government sent army reinforcements to Algeria. While the French military kept firm control of the Algerian Sahara, the independence movement gained a large following in Muslim cities and villages in the north. Other North African nations, including Egypt, Morocco, and Tunisia, pledged their support to the FLN.

In the late 1950s, the FLN brought the revolt to France, where bombings and assassinations occurred in cafes and in other public places. As violence spread

After World War II ended, the Algerian drive for independence brought about a long and bloody civil war. By 1961 the fighting in Algeria had driven thousands of refugees into border camps in both Tunisia and Morocco. Many parents who sent their children to these camps stayed behind in Algeria to protect their homes and property.

Courtesy of UN High Commissioner for Refugees/S. Wright

35

within Algeria, the French military took drastic measures to put down the revolt. French planes bombed Muslim towns and villages, and many people suspected of helping the FLN were placed in guarded camps. The discovery of large oil reserves in the Sahara Desert during the 1950s gave the French another reason to fight for control of Algeria.

As the conflict continued, many French leaders began pressing for a settlement with representatives of Algeria's Muslims. Several French officers in Algeria, however, opposed any negotiations between the two sides. In May 1958, these officers staged a revolt, taking over government buildings in Algiers. Unable to defeat the rebellion, the French government lost support and fell from power. In the summer of 1958, General Charles de Gaulle, a commander of French forces during World War II, became the new president of France.

By the early 1960s, French president Charles de Gaulle realized that his country's forces could not defeat the widespread uprising against French rule in Algeria. De Gaulle's government agreed to self-rule for Algeria in the spring of 1962.

De Gaulle proved to be a strong leader, but support for the war in Algeria steadily declined in France. In 1959 de Gaulle stated that Algerian Muslims should have the right to elect their own government. In response, many colons who were violently opposed to this position formed private militias. These forces carried out attacks on Muslims and on the French armed forces.

International pressure on the French government for a settlement of the conflict increased in the early 1960s. As the war dragged on, French leaders saw that they could not maintain control over the vast territory of Algeria or over its majority Muslim population.

Independence and FLN Rule

In March 1962, the French government met with FLN representatives in Evian, Switzerland. The two sides agreed to a cease-fire and to the right of Algerians to decide their own future. A referendum (public vote) held among Algerians in July resulted in a formal declaration of independence on July 3, 1962.

In September the new National Constituent Assembly proclaimed the founding of the Democratic and Popular Republic of Algeria. Ahmed Ben Bella, the founder of the FLN, became the republic's first prime minister. The vast majority of colons, as well as many Muslims who had supported the French in the conflict, left the country after independence.

Algerians faced the difficult task of creating a new government and restoring damaged industries and cities. The FLN passed laws that made it the only legal political party in the country. Delegates to the assembly had to be chosen from a list of FLN members. Ben Bella also proclaimed Algeria a socialist state, in which workers would manage industries and farms.

The Algerian economy was strictly controlled by the government, which took over foreign businesses, banks, mines, fac-

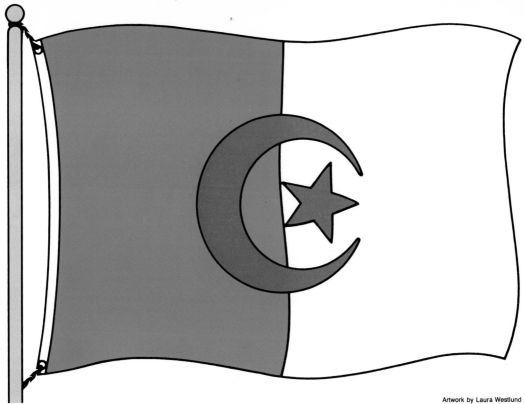

Artwork by Laura Westlund

Most historians agree that, during the 1920s, Ahmed Messali Hadj designed what would become the modern Algerian flag. The National Liberation Front (FLN), the ruling party in Algeria, adopted the flag as its official standard in 1948, 14 years before Algeria's independence from France. The star and crescent were traditional symbols of the Ottoman Empire. Green and white—standing for fertility and purity, respectively—are common colors in the flags of Islamic nations.

tories, and retail stores. Land once owned by Europeans was turned over to committees of farm workers. These policies failed to raise productivity, and many inefficient worker-run factories eventually were put under direct government management.

An authoritarian leader, Ben Bella personally controlled the armed forces and most government ministries. He aligned Algeria with the Soviet Union, then a powerful socialist nation, and declared his support for independence movements within European colonies in Africa. Algeria also became a leader of colonies that had become independent since World War II. Many Algerians disagreed with Ben Bella's economic and foreign policies, however, and some government officials formed opposition groups.

Houari Boumediene, a hero of the war for independence, led the largest opposi-

tion group. He felt that Ben Bella's strict rule was hurting Algeria's chances for a full recovery from the years of conflict with France. After gaining the support of several ministers and army officers, Boumediene deposed Ben Bella in June 1965.

Boumediene's government dissolved the assembly, suspended the constitution, and set up a ruling council of 26 members. The council was designed to bring a greater range of approaches to Algeria's problems. The new president, who governed the country by decree, focused on improving the economy. Algeria hired skilled technicians to run state-owned industries. The government also financed new projects with income from the export of Algeria's reserves of oil and natural gas.

In the early 1970s, Algeria nationalized—or took over from private owners—its oil industry. Boumediene favored using his

Courtesy of Embassy of Algeria

In the 1980s, President Chadli Bendjedid attempted to improve the Algerian economy by transferring more state-owned firms to private ownership. But economic and political instability prompted Algeria's military to force Bendjedid's resignation in January 1992.

country's abundant natural resources to achieve Algeria's political and economic goals. Algeria became an important supporter of an embargo (ban) on the export of oil from Arab countries in 1973. This action caused the price of oil, and the value of oil reserves, to rise sharply. Algeria also became a founding member of the Organization of African Unity (OAU), an association that pursues agreements among independent African nations.

In 1976, to strengthen FLN control of the government, Boumediene proposed a new constitution that would create a National People's Assembly of 261 FLN members. By a nearly unanimous vote, Algerian voters approved the changes. But in December 1978 Boumediene died of a rare blood disease. In January 1979, the FLN chose Chadli Bendjedid, one of Boumediene's aides and a respected military commander, as the country's new president.

Recent Events

To improve Algeria's weak economy, Bendjedid lessened government ownership of Algerian industries. A five-year plan for the economy adopted in 1980 called for the breakup of large companies into smaller, more independent businesses. The government ended its strict control over farming and rural land ownership. Bendjedid also attempted to stop corruption among government officials, a problem that was causing waste and inefficiency in the Algerian economy.

Bendjedid's reforms did not prevent unrest in 1980 and 1981 among Berber-speaking peoples, many of whom have a long history of self-rule within Algeria. In Algiers and in the city of Tizi-Ouzou, Berber students protested the decline of Berber-language education in Algerian universities. When the government agreed to make changes, violent clashes broke out between Muslims and Berbers. Despite the violence and continuing economic problems, Algerians elected Bendjedid to additional terms as president in 1984 and 1988.

In 1991 demonstrations again broke out in the capital of Algiers. Members of the Islamic Salvation Front (FIS), demanding government reform along Islamic religious principles, gained decisive victories in legislative elections. In January 1992, Bendjedid resigned under pressure from military leaders who feared an FIS majority in the Algerian legislature. A five-member High State Council then postponed elections and assumed the duties of the ousted president.

The country's economic weakness has persisted into the early 1990s. Manufacturing businesses suffer from low productivity, and farms are unable to grow enough crops to feed the expanding population. In addition, population growth and the migration of rural people to the cities of northern Algeria have put great strains on the country's educational and social systems. These issues, and continuing antigovernment violence, threaten to end the FLN's hold on Algeria's economy and legislature.

Government

The Algerian republic is based on a constitution drawn up in 1976. Since independence, Algeria's government has been in the hands of the FLN. Once the country's only legal political party, the FLN amended the Algerian constitution in the late 1980s to allow opposition parties.

Although Chadli Bendjedid won election to the presidency in 1988, he has been replaced by a High State Council which now directs defense and foreign affairs. Under the Algerian constitution, Algeria's president is normally elected to a five-year term by a vote of citizens over the age of 18. The president appoints a prime minis-ter, who has the power to draw up legislation and to appoint a council of ministers. The 26 members of this cabinet supervise the various government ministries. Voters also elect the 295 members of the National People's Assembly to five-year terms.

The supreme court is the country's highest court of appeal. Lower courts sit in Algiers, Oran, and Constantine, and there are 48 provincial courts. Local tribunals hear criminal and civil cases.

Algeria is divided into 48 provinces known as *wilayat.* The federal government appoints the wilaya governors. There are also 691 communes—cities, towns, and villages. Each wilaya and each commune is governed by an elected assembly. Municipal councils in Algeria's cities pass local laws, elect mayors, and appoint civil administrators.

Photo by Reuters/Bettmann

Children play among the debris of a government store that angry crowds attacked in 1988. Bread shortages and high prices at public food markets touched off rioting in Algiers and in other Algerian cities.

Street vendors in Oran sell a variety of fruits and vegetables that farmers raise on nearby lands.

3) The People

Algeria, Africa's second largest nation in area, has a population of 26 million. The country's high growth rate of 2.7 percent, although average for North Africa, has caused a shortage of housing and school classrooms. Overcrowding has become a serious problem in many cities, and Algerian farms can supply only a small percentage of the food needed by the growing population. Algeria's government supports a national program to control population growth through family planning.

About half of all Algerians now live in the Tell region, where there are large cities, farming estates, industries, and harbors. Settlement in the dry plains south of the Tell is sparse. In the Saharan Atlas Moun-

tains and in the country's vast desert interior, population densities have always been extremely low.

Since independence, many of the country's rural inhabitants have moved northward to cities along the Mediterranean coast, causing a decline in the population of villages and small towns. In addition, more than one million Algerians have emigrated to Europe—especially to France—in search of work.

Ethnic Groups

Most modern Algerians are descendants of North African Berbers, but Berber and Arab peoples have been mixing within

Algerian society since the Arab invasions of the seventh century. Berber-speaking peoples now make up about 20 percent of the nation's population, and communities made up solely of Berber-speakers still exist in many parts of Algeria. Arabs and Berbers generally have equal access to jobs, housing, and services in Algerian cities.

The Arab conquest of North Africa in the seventh century brought the Arabic language and customs to much of northern Algeria. Unlike the nomadic Berbers, the Arabs formed a settled urban population. Gradually the Berber peoples of the desert and rural areas adopted Islam, the religion of the Arab invaders. Their faith gave Arabs and Berbers a common identity as Muslims during the conflict with the largely Roman Catholic Algerian colons.

Many of Algeria's Berber groups have remained independent of the country's

Courtesy of Arab World Ministries

This child's clothing protects him from the intense sunlight and heat of the desert, where temperatures can reach 120° F. Desert dwellers also wear robes and head wraps to guard against high winds, dust, and sand.

Photo © John Chitty/Root Resources

A musician entertains a crowd with the sounds of a *rhita,* or reed flute.

Arab society. These groups include Kabyle Berbers, who became an important class of merchants during the French occupation. Originally from the Kabylia Mountains east of Algiers, the Kabyles have established new communities in other parts of the country. The Chaouia Berbers live in the Aurès Mountains near Constantine. The seven walled cities of the Mzab region in the northern Sahara are home to the Mzab people, who have maintained their separate culture within Algeria for more than 1,000 years.

Farther south, nomadic groups employed as herders and guides populate the Algerian Sahara. The Tuareg people live in southern Algeria as well as in Mali and Niger. Able to move freely across national boundaries, Tuareg caravans travel in search of water, pasture, and game. Many of the Tuareg have adopted a more settled life in the oases and scattered towns of southern Algeria.

After independence, most of the non-Muslim colonists living in Algeria left the country. Of the 100,000 Europeans who remain, about 45,000 are of French heritage. Many Europeans work in the cities as engineers, teachers, and civil servants.

Language

The majority of Algerians speak Arabic, the country's official language. This Middle Eastern tongue spread slowly through the region after the Arab conquest and was closely tied to the conversion of Algerians to the Islamic religion. Classical Arabic gradually became an international language of scholars, scientists, and writers living throughout North Africa and the Middle East.

Two forms of modern Arabic – literary Arabic and dialectical (conversational) Arabic—are in use in modern Algeria. A simpler version of classical Arabic, literary Arabic is used in newspapers, in many books, and in political speeches. Dialectical Arabic is the everyday language spoken by Algerians.

Many Algerians, and all of the country's European people, can read and speak French. Algerians in business and government often use French to communicate and negotiate. Some newspapers are written in French, but since independence Arabic has replaced French as the language of the courts and schools.

Over the centuries, many words have been exchanged between the Arabic and Berber languages. A number of Berber dialects, including Kabyle and Chaouia, have survived in rural areas where Berber-speakers remain the majority population. In addition, the Tuareg and Mzab peoples speak their own version of the Berber language. Some Berbers also use a distinctive alphabet for written records and for official documents.

Photo by Bernice K. Condit

Berber women wait for health care in a clinic in Bordj Bou Arreridj, a predominantly Berber town in the Kabylia Mountains of northern Algeria.

These girls attend an elementary school in Algiers. The public school system in Algeria underwent a complete overhaul in 1976, when Arabic replaced French as the language of education.

Education

In 1976 Algeria abolished the country's private, French-language schools and began a complete reform of the educational system. By law, children between the ages of 6 and 15 are required to attend school. Primary school lasts for six years, and students enroll in a secondary school for an additional four years. About one-third of Algerian students then continue their studies in a three-year high school program.

The Algerian government has increased its financial support of the nation's schools. The state places its greatest emphasis on teacher training, on adult literacy, and on technical and scientific courses of study. The government also supports vocational and technical training. Despite these efforts, nearly 20 percent of Algeria's children do not attend school, and only about 45 percent of the population can read and write.

Algeria has eight universities, the largest of which is the University of Algiers. Opened in 1879, this institution enrolls more than 15,000 students and has separate schools of law, medicine, science, and the liberal arts.

Religion

Islam, the religion of most Algerians, has been an important factor in Algerian history and society for more than a thousand years. The word *Islam* means "submission to the will of Allah." Muslims believe that the word of God (Allah) was revealed to the prophet Muhammad in the Koran, which is the basis for Islamic laws.

43

Devout Muslims pray five times a day, sometimes in mosques (Islamic houses of prayer). During the month of Ramadan, Muslims observe a fast, taking only water between sunrise and sunset. Muslim believers are also required to make a pilgrimage to the holy city of Mecca in Saudi Arabia at least once during their lifetimes, if they are able.

Muhammad saw Islam as a guide for both civic and spiritual life. Since independence, the Algerian government has integrated many of the religion's principles into the country's laws and administration. The government also financially supports Algeria's 5,000 mosques and pays for the training of Muslim clergy. Nevertheless, many fundamentalists, who favor a more strict observance of Islam, are pressing Algeria's leaders for further reform along religious lines.

The government allows non-Islamic religions, such as Roman Catholicism, to exist in Algeria. Most of the European inhabitants of Algeria are members of the Catholic church.

Health and Social Welfare

Overcrowding, poor sanitation, and a lack of food—especially in rural areas—cause many of Algeria's health problems. The most serious illnesses are tuberculosis and trachoma (an eye disease). The infant mortality rate—or the number of babies who die within the first year of life—is 74 per 1,000 births, and life expectancy is 64 years. These rates are better in Algeria than in other countries of the Maghrib and of the western Sahara.

Since 1974 medical care has been free for all Algerian citizens. The government con-

The Jema el-Jedid mosque in Algiers, which dates to the early seventeenth century, rises in the Place of the Martyrs, a large public square. The city's architects built the square as a memorial to the Algerians who died in the war for independence from French rule.

Young men learn crafts at an orphan's center near the town of Tizi-Ouzou.

tinues to build new clinics in rural areas that lack medical facilities and doctors. Algerian physicians, dentists, and pharmacists are required to spend five years in the public health service, after which they may apply for licenses to practice privately. Foreign medical professionals and medical students also staff Algeria's rural clinics.

The Algerian government provides benefits for the aged, the poor, and the disabled. Sickness and disability insurance cover the country's workers, who also collect pensions when they retire. The government pays allowances to families, depending on the number of children in the family. Taxes on employers and employees support these benefits.

The Arts

Ancient Roman and Byzantine inhabitants left a rich architectural legacy in Algeria. The ruins of many Roman cities —with their arches, stadiums, homes, and statues—lie near the Mediterranean coast. Algerian builders used both Roman and Byzantine features in mosques built after the Arab conquest. For example, the Jema el-Jedid mosque in Algiers follows the plan

Founded during the 1800s, this *zaouïa* – or religious sanctuary – is at El Hamel. Islamic pilgrims come from long distances to visit the zaouïa, which has become an important center of religious worship and study.

Photo by Daniel H. Condit

Architects designed elaborate interiors *(above)* and exteriors *(below)* for these mosques in the Maghrib. Islam prohibits representations of people or animals, so artists used intricate geometric motifs to decorate doorways, walls, ceilings, and towers.

Independent Picture Service

of a Byzantine church in the city of Istanbul, which was the capital of the Byzantine and Ottoman empires. Many Algerian architects were also influenced by the decorative arts of Andalusia, the region of southern Spain once ruled by the Islamic Moors.

Algerian mosques, traditionally designed to resemble the house of Muhammad, have many features in common. Four walls surround a central courtyard, and a hall for prayer stands on one side of the mosque. A tall minaret (tower), from which the faithful are called to prayer, rises from a corner of the structure. Many mosques also have a large dome that covers the building's central hall.

Since Islam forbids drawings of figures and animals in religious art, mosque interiors often display elaborate geometric designs that cover the ceilings and walls. Intricate wood and stone carvings also decorate many Algerian civic buildings and palaces. Many modern Algerian artists have drawn on traditional Islamic motifs in their works.

Algeria's literature began in religious writings produced by the nation's Islamic scholars. Before the country's independence, many Algerian writers used French. Albert Camus, an Algerian of European ancestry, was an essayist, playwright, and novelist who won the Nobel Prize for literature in 1957. Many of Camus's works, including *The Stranger* and *The Plague,* describe the author's pessimistic philosophy of modern people and society. After independence, Algeria's writers and artists rejected European ideas and turned for inspiration to the country's Arabic and Islamic traditions. Mohammed Dib, a noted Muslim author, has written plays, poetry, and novels describing the lives and struggles of rural Algerians.

Courtesy of Editions du Seuil/Photo Lutfi Ozkök

Mohammed Dib, born in 1920 in Tlemcen, has published nearly two dozen works, including novels, poetry, and plays. His career spans a tumultuous period of Algerian history, when civil war and modernization brought great changes to the Algerians.

Courtesy of French Embassy Press & Information Division

The Algerian writer and philosopher Albert Camus, who wrote in French, became one of the most influential figures of European literature in the years after World War II.

Algerian cooks can select their ingredients from the wide range of food and spices that farmers offer for sale in the country's towns and villages.

Food

Algeria shares its traditional cuisine with Morocco and Tunisia, neighboring countries of the Maghrib. A North African dish known as *couscous* is a popular meal in all parts of Algeria. To make couscous, cooks sprinkle oil and water on semolina (a by-product of milling hard wheat), then roll it into tiny morsels. The pieces are then steamed and covered with a thick, spicy tomato sauce. The sauce may contain vegetables and fish, beef, or mutton (the meat of sheep).

Main courses include roast mutton and lamb, which are often grilled on a spit, as well as chicken stuffed with almonds, raisins, and rice. Various soups have gained favor in Algeria's large cities. *Chorba beida*, popular in both large cities and in the countryside, is chicken soup with vegetables, pasta, and egg yolk. *Harissa*, a hot seasoning of red pepper, salt, and garlic, often accompanies soups made from lentils and beans. Mediterranean seafood served in Algeria includes bass, perch, mullet, and sole.

Sweet desserts of *baklava* and *khtayef* consist of nuts, honey, and sugar, combined in a thin pastry. Many Algerians enjoy a glass of sweet mint tea or coffee after meals. French colonists first brought wine grapes to northern Algeria in the nineteenth century. Since then Algerian wines have gained an international reputation. Many of the country's strong red wines, including Médéa and Lismara, are popular in Europe. Rosé wines are also produced in the Tell region.

Sports and Recreation

Many young Algerians are enthusiastic participants in recreational and competitive sports. Amateur and school teams play soccer (known in Algeria as football), the country's most popular sport. The Algerian national soccer team has participated in championships held by the African Football Confederation.

Algerians have also competed in the international Olympic Games. Alain Mimoun —an Algerian runner who represented France in the 1948, 1952, and 1956 games —won silver medals in several long-distance races and a gold medal in the 1956 Olympic marathon.

Algeria's sports facilities include a golf course near Algiers, indoor and outdoor swimming pools, tennis courts, and ski resorts. Water-skiing and sailing clubs operate in resorts along the Mediterranean Sea. Both Algerians and tourists enjoy horseback riding, mountaineering, and camping.

Courtesy of Lothar Rübelt/International Olympic Committee

Alain Mimoun *(right),* **an Algerian athlete competing for the French Olympic team, won the silver medal in the 5,000-meter race during the Summer Olympics of 1952 in Helsinki. Because it was considered a part of France at the time, Algeria did not field an Olympic team of its own.**

Since the 1950s, oil has provided Algeria with most of its foreign earnings. At this work site in the eastern Sahara, welders prepare a pipeline that will transport oil to refineries along Algeria's Mediterranean coast.

4) The Economy

Algeria's economy made a slow recovery after the civil war that ended in 1962. The conflict damaged or destroyed many towns, farms, and industries. In addition, skilled workers, technicians, and business managers left the country immediately after independence. These factors made rebuilding the economy a difficult task for the new Algerian leadership.

Since 1962 the FLN government has nationalized major industries, services, banks, mining companies, and many farming estates. By this action, the government hoped to foster economic recovery while controlling prices, wages, and production. Algeria heavily taxed workers and businesses to pay for new job benefits and social services. But nationalization

Many suqs contain dozens of shops offering items created by Algeria's craftspeople. People use baskets sold at this suq in Bordj Bou Arreridj to transport goods by hand and on the backs of work animals.

Trucks, cars, and pedestrians crowd the main street of this village in the Sahara Desert. The desert settlements are important rest stops for truckers and tourists who must navigate the vast distances of the desert.

and high taxes discouraged foreign companies from investing in Algerian firms.

Despite its weak economy, Algeria gained income throughout the 1960s and 1970s by exporting crude oil and natural gas. This money enabled the government to develop new industries and to begin increasing food production in the 1980s. After coming to power in 1979, President Chadli Bendjedid sought to improve the economy by lessening government controls over state-owned businesses. Bendjedid also lowered taxes on small, privately owned firms.

Allowed to operate and compete more freely, many Algerian companies began to prosper. Others continued to lose money through inefficiency and outdated methods and equipment. In the late 1980s and early 1990s, high unemployment and food shortages caused strikes and violent demonstrations. Continuing public unrest has put pressure on the Algerian government to make further economic reforms.

Courtesy of FAO

Workers plant saplings in plastic bags of specially prepared soil, then cover the beds with split reed mats. Later, the workers will replant the trees in the open desert to fight soil erosion.

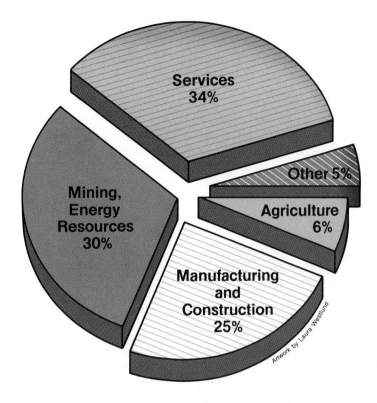

Manufacturing

Manufacturing makes up about one-fourth of Algeria's total production of goods. The government controls most of the heavy industries, such as steelmaking, oil refining, and chemical production. Export earnings helped the FLN regime to invest in new factories and equipment during the 1980s. Modernization efforts, however, have closed some inefficient plants and caused the loss of manufacturing jobs.

Nearly all of Algeria's heavy industries are located on or near the Mediterranean coast. Ironworks and steelworks in the largest cities provide export income, as well as materials for new apartments and commercial buildings. Other plants produce fertilizers, plastics, and chemicals from the by-products of crude oil. Large refineries near the Mediterranean coast process oil and natural gas.

Smaller firms—which are more likely to be privately owned—make furniture, plastic goods, textiles, and finished clothing.

Food-processing companies produce olive oil, tobacco, and Algerian wine, much of which is exported to France and other European countries.

Energy and Mining

Algeria's reserves of crude oil and natural gas provide the country with inexpensive sources of energy. Oil and gas products are also Algeria's most valuable exports. After oil was discovered in the eastern Sahara in 1956, French-owned companies built a network of wells, refineries, and pipelines in Algeria.

Although many French engineers left Algeria after independence in 1962, the French and Algerian governments continued to cooperate in oil exploration and drilling. In 1971 the FLN government nationalized the country's oil industry. Income from the sale of energy products abroad has since helped Algeria to develop other sectors of the economy.

In scattered locations in the Sahara Desert, underground water sources will support an oasis—an area of date palms and natural vegetation. At the oasis of Timimoun in the Great Western Erg, an irrigation canal directs water to a palm plantation.

Photo © Irma Turtle

Courtesy of FAO

Drought has killed both crops and animals in large areas of the southern Sahara.

Algeria also has extensive reserves of iron ore, the raw material for finished iron and steel products. In addition, companies extract phosphates from mines near Algeria's border with Tunisia. The phosphates are then made into agricultural fertilizer. Other important mineral resources include lead, zinc, mercury, salt, and uranium. Reserves of coal exist near the northern Saharan city of Béchar.

Agriculture, Fishing, and Forestry

Many of Algeria's large farming estates became the property of the government during the 1960s. The management of the farms was turned over to laborers who had once worked for colon landowners. The FLN, however, favored the development of industry and energy resources over agricultural reform. Another setback was the drought and erosion of the 1980s,

54

which destroyed some productive land. As a result, farm production in Algeria declined steadily. The situation has caused food shortages and has forced the country to import most of its food.

In the 1980s, the government allowed many farmers to buy the land they worked. Others were offered free plots in exchange for a promise to cultivate the land. For the first time since independence, laws permitted private food markets. Growers seeking better prices and more efficient distribution of their goods formed marketing cooperatives, which also allow members to share equipment and supplies. By the early 1990s, successful farm cooperatives had begun to increase the country's production of food.

Most of Algeria's farmable land lies on or near the Mediterranean coastline. Wheat, barley, and oats are the principal

United Nations Photo by Ruth Massey

Farm workers cultivate pea plants near the town of Saïda, which lies 200 miles southwest of Algiers.

Courtesy of Arab World Ministries

Agricultural production declined in Algeria during the 1980s, when many Algerian farmers still lacked modern equipment. Near Cherchell, this farmer uses traditional techniques of planting, cultivating, and harvesting his crops.

grain crops. Also suited to the warm, dry climate of the Tell region are citrus fruits, vegetables, wine grapes, and olive trees. In the oases of the Sahara, farmers grow grains and vegetables on small plots. Plantations of date palms are common in the oases and near desert water sources. Algeria has become one of the world's leading exporters of dates.

Animal diseases and the loss of pasturage reduced the number of livestock in Algeria during the 1970s. Herders still raise sheep and goats on uncultivated land in the north, as well as in the lower elevations of the Saharan Atlas. Farmers also raise cattle for dairy production and camels and donkeys as work animals.

Algeria has both private fishing operations and government-run cooperatives that fish in the Mediterranean Sea. Tuna, sardines, bluefish, and shellfish are sold on the domestic market. A lack of commercial trucking, however, prevents much of the Mediterranean catch from reaching consumers who live south of the coastal region.

Loggers have cut down many of Algeria's pine, cedar, and oak trees for building materials and for firewood. Sawn timber supplies the construction industry, and Algerian farmers harvest cork from cork oak trees. The government, which has begun reforestation and conservation efforts, now owns about one-half of the country's forests. But centuries of unrestricted logging has reduced forested areas to only about 1 percent of Algeria's total land area.

Courtesy of FAO

Workers clear weeds from around young trees that have been planted as part of Algeria's reforestation program.

This suspension bridge is one of four spans crossing the deep ravines that cut through the city of Constantine.

Transportation

Algeria's colon administrators built an extensive road network in the country's northern provinces before the war for independence. About 50,000 miles of roads in the Tell and along the coast now connect Algeria's cities, towns, and ports. A railroad system runs from the Mediterranean Sea southward to towns in the northern Sahara. A rail line also links Mediterranean ports and remote oil fields in the eastern Sahara. Buses serve many of the country's smaller towns and villages.

The Trans-Saharan Highway, a road running from north to south across the Sahara Desert, has become a principal route for tourists and for trucks that carry goods between the nations of northern and western Africa. Despite this highway, many isolated oases cannot be reached by Algeria's road or rail networks.

Automobiles and farmers' carts share a tree-lined street in Bordj Bou Arreridj.

Travelers need hardy all-terrain vehicles to navigate the rough tracks of the southern Sahara. Spare tires—and extra food and water—are essential, because towns and supplies are sometimes hundreds of miles apart.

Air Algerie, the national airline, flies domestic and international routes. Eight international airports are operating, the largest of which is near Algiers. Other major airports provide an important link to the towns and oases of the south, which are difficult to reach over land. The country has large seaports at Algiers and Oran. The busy port of Annaba handles many of Algeria's industrial and oil exports.

Trade and Tourism

Huge oil and natural gas reserves supply nearly 90 percent of Algeria's exports. The country is a member of the Organization of Petroleum Exporting Countries (OPEC). This association of oil-producing nations sets production quotas among its members. In 1973 Algeria led an OPEC embargo that caused oil prices to rise. Since then the country has maintained a small trade surplus, meaning that the value of Algeria's exports exceeds the value of its imports. The United States is Algeria's largest customer for energy products.

Other important Algerian exports include citrus fruits, iron ore, phosphates, tobacco, cork, and wine. Algeria's principal imports are machinery, raw materials, food, iron, steel, and textiles. Italy, Germany, and Japan have become important trading partners for Algeria. Since the nineteenth century, France has been the biggest buyer of Algerian wine. French companies have also invested in Algerian businesses and industries.

During the years after independence, Algeria did little to encourage foreign visitors. The government did not begin to develop the tourist industry until the 1980s. By the end of the decade, tourists

Photo by Liba Taylor/The Hutchison Library

Much of Algeria's foreign trade passes through the port of Algiers, where international cargo ships dock to take on and discharge their goods.

The city of Tlemcen, once the capital of the Zayanid dynasty in western Algeria, still has impressive walls and fortifications that date from the thirteenth century.

A young boy takes charge of a team of camels. Tourists pay to ride the animals within the towns and oases of the Sahara Desert.

The ruins of this Christian basilica (church) have survived since the fourth century in Tipasa, on the Mediterranean coast. Tipasa was an important Phoenician and Roman trading city and now attracts many visitors who are interested in archaeological sites.

Photo by Jaap Verschoor, Haarlem, the Netherlands

were spending about $140 million a year in the country. New hotels and resorts have been built along the seacoast to take advantage of Algeria's sunny climate and extensive Mediterranean beaches. These resorts attract many northern Europeans, who seek warm weather during the harsh winters in their own countries.

Many tourists also visit Algeria's archaeological sites. These include the ruins of ancient Roman and Carthaginian cities in the Tell. Another popular attraction is a large area of Stone Age rock paintings in the Tassili N'Ajjer region of the southeastern Sahara. Tlemcen has religious and civic buildings built by the wealthy Berber dynasties that made the city an economic and cultural center. The traditional architecture and culture of the oases of the Sahara—which can be easily reached by air—are also drawing an increasing number of tourists.

Photo by Daniel H. Condit

Architects designed these homes in Constantine with traditional small balconies, shaded porches, and arched doorways.

This farmer is inspecting his vineyards in Médéa, where winegrowers produce and bottle Algeria's most famous wines.

The Future

Despite a trade surplus and income from its reserves of oil and natural gas, Algeria has made slow progress in improving its economy. Algerians continue to experience urban overcrowding, high unemployment, and occasional food shortages.

President Bendjedid made efforts to spur economic growth by loosening government controls, but the Algerian economy still suffers from inefficiency. In addition, Algeria has had difficulty attracting the foreign investors it needs to modernize its industries.

Algeria's political future is also uncertain. After 30 years of FLN leadership, opposing parties scored decisive election victories in the early 1990s. The Islamic Salvation Front (FIS)—the most popular opposition party—seeks to reshape Algerian society strictly according to the principles of Islam.

Many Algerians who are frustrated with the FLN have elected FIS members to run town councils and provincial governments. Others fear the sweeping social changes that could occur if the military or the FIS manages to take control of the Algerian government. Algeria's future depends on the ability of its leaders and opposition groups to cooperate in addressing the nation's economic problems.

A parade of camels and their riders passes a crowd at a festival in Metlili Chaamba, a town in the Mzab region.

Residents in both modern and traditional clothing mingle in this Saharan village. The contrast in dress reflects a deeper division within Algeria, where many favor a return to Islamic values to solve the country's economic and social problems.

Index